Railwalker

POEMS

JEANINE RENÉE

RAILWALKER: POEMS

Published by Tar Paper Media
Paonia, CO

Copyright ©2023 by Jeanine Renée. All rights reserved.

Website: jeaninerenee.com

No part of this book may be reproduced in any form or by any mechanical means, including information storage and retrieval systems without permission in writing from the publisher/author, except by a reviewer who may quote passages in a review.

All images, logos, quotes, and trademarks included in this book are subject to use according to trademark and copyright laws of the United States of America.

ISBN: 979-8-218-24930-4 (pbk)

POETRY / General

Cover art by Behind The Rocks Studio.

Cover and Layout Design by Asya Blue Design copyright owned by Jeanine Renée.

QUANTITY PURCHASES: Schools, companies, professional groups, clubs, and other organizations may qualify for special terms when ordering quantities of this title. For information, email jeanine@tarpapermedia.com.

All rights reserved by Jeanine Renée and Tar Paper Media.

Printed in the United States of America.

To My Lou

The rumble of your laughter stirs my earth…

Daffodils spring to my lips.

Contents

On the Cusp 1

Consequence 3

Echoes 5

Rock Me 7

Utterance 9

Language of Women 11

Grief 13

May 15

Paramour 17

Barbara 19

Nothing to be Done 21

Denial 23

White Pick-up and a Loaded Gun 24

So…I Walk the Rails 27

Resolute 29

Ahhh… 31

S'il Vous Plaît 33

And So, We Begin 35

First Night 37

Set to Rights 39

Do Not Touch 41

Making for Home 43

Ease 45

The Parting 46

Truce? 47

Too Tight 49

Sleight of Hand 51

Let Me Entertain You 53

Sweet Rebellion 55

Quashed Coup 57

Earth Mother 59

Communion 61

Reset 63

Freeze Frame 65

Hard Lesson 67

Proof of Life 69

Samaritan 71

Shadow Life 73

Tattered 75

Secret 77

Pleasures 79

Mystic Morning 81

Turn, Turn, Turn 83

Musings 85

Nature's Retreat 87

Tender Trust 89

The Biding 91

Spring Lamb 93

Sing to Me 95

Magnificent One 97

Railwalker

On the Cusp

Perched here on this edge

I wait for a single subtle breeze,

vital, irresistible…

to fill these folded wings

that I might ferociously surrender.

Consequence

I no longer recognize this well-worn path I trod.

Intersecting livestock trails and rain

have altered the terrain.

I no longer trust where this way will lead.

Dusk disorients and confuses.

The setting sun backlights,

exposing what I would not see.

A child within pauses and silently mourns –

there is no way but forward.

Echoes

I carry a song in my pocket

that I sing along the ditch –

It holds a piece of my past

locked within its resonant mourning.

A cry echoes forth

from the broken hobo's journey

caked in sin

like the tar on a rail walker's shoes.

Rock Me

We are the walkers –

lonely souls walking alleys,

ditch banks and rail tracks –

poetry and songs heaving

from the dirt beneath our feet.

Searching for answers to questions

our lips have not yet formed,

our quest eternally elusive

pulling us onward

even as we rest –

rocked by the rhythm of our steps,

the repetition of the rails.

Utterance

Faces and impressions of people – I never knew –

create shadow and texture of untold stories.

Why does the player in my head strike their notes

opening rivulets of melodious memory?

A melancholy old as the earth beneath my feet

bides in my blood coloring the chords.

A voice I know – but have never heard –

directs my voice as if it were not my own.

I weep not for myself alone – but for the silenced –

whose blood I carry and ground I have inhabited…

cries that pool in my soul until the story is told.

Language of Women

In your eyes I see the cost of courage.

In the curl of your smile –

the weight of your grief,

and mine rise to meet you.

Looking into each other's eyes

there is understanding without words.

Another irretrievable loss.

Another devastation.

Another moment to stand here with each other

as the earth shifts beneath us,

as we get our bearings –

as the well of courage replenishes.

My Friend, we will do this again I fear –

Hopefully not soon.

Grief

This open wound which cannot be stemmed,

continues to seep long after the strike.

Refusing to close and heal,

reminding the bereft they are not whole

and cannot pretend to be.

A solitary journey, no well-intentioned Prophet

should presume to predict.

Humbling, this common malady

for which we have no language…

for which we have no cure.

May

Summer lies before me as a sweet promise,

scented with turned soil, rosemary, and fresh cut hay.

Anticipation of family meals buttered with laughter

softens the annual pang of losing you.

A hint of your perfume resurrects primal sensations

wrapped in the soft bosom of your embrace.

Paramour

You approach with tenderness

caressing with unearthly hues,

the soft underside of morning.

Your cool breath, a herald,

scattering my hair.

I close my eyes

as your brilliance crests the peak,

warms my skin – stirring my soul.

You have come again my faithful lover

easing this abiding loneliness.

Barbara

Threads…

Interwoven memories – one after another

work themselves into my consciousness

tickling my lips into a smile

even as the ache in my heart

draws tears down my cheeks.

Inseverable…the love you sewed into the lining

of a young woman's soul.

Nothing to be Done

My children are scattered across a troubled world.

Rain drives me inside from the solace that is my garden,

where a storm within casts its shadow across my best intentions.

I search but cannot find my sense of humor or my keys.

Staring out the window…for how long now?

My thoughts land and splatter with the raindrops on the pane.

Dis-ease, fueled by bold conflicting political assertions

fans the fire in my blood…lowering the blinds soothes me.

Perhaps retreat for restoration is the brave choice today.

Denial

In this room there is a draft.

I raise my collar, palm this flame and move to another.

My house has many rooms.

White Pick-up and a Loaded Gun

It never leaves.

Years filled with days

create an illusion of distance – easily overrun.

That crisp November evening

a vibrant self-reliant student

walked out of her before

into a collision of free wills.

White pick-up and a loaded gun

standing in the way

of all forward motion –

Past and Future eclipsed.

Cage on wheels.

No combination of words opened the door.

He took what was not his –

So began the terror of my vigil…

>Still as the hare.
>
>Planning. Praying.
>
>Yes. I can hold my breath for hours.
>
>Cold. Cold to the bone
>
>Silent…invisible.
>
>Long odds – escape – by inches.
>
>Running…hiding.
>
>A wary, panicked freedom.

…As another self

in a beautiful life

I am sporadically reminded

through unpredictable throes of flight –

Dark scenarios once remote

now reside in my mind's reality

Not inevitable of course –

I'm not crazy.

So…I Walk the Rails

Future uncertain

Vast dark unspeakable edge

Lonely hurtling through space

Don't ask what I need

Just stand close so I can breathe

Your touch will bruise me

Please do not see me

Let me pass as a ghost

Walking through her pain

Feather on the ground

Above this earth you soared

Tell me what you've seen

Oh, my sister soul

To know you whole once again

Home return to me

So…I walk the rails

As the dusk shadows lengthen

Each mile a mending

Resolute

Fragments of tormented dreams

scratch trails across my semi-conscious mind –

annoyingly just out of focus.

Dissonant melodies fall into rhythm,

only to slip away and be forgotten.

The past, uninvited, inserts itself

in this most unguarded of moments,

beating its chest, pointing its finger,

demanding accountability.

Diminished – I toss and turn,

wrestling with this weight of self-loathing.

A contra dance of memories

rush in…rush out…rush in again.

Each dancer piling on their version of the facts

till I can no longer move.

Grasping consciousness,

I remind myself once more this morning –

"Surrender Only To The Truth!"

Deafening the sound…

as the burden falls from shoulder to ground.

Ahhh...

I throw off this weight

Like so many covers on a midsummer night

S'il Vous Plaît

I made a window where there was none –

to watch the birds in the morning

I opened a door once nailed shut –

for my soul to come and go

I invited music

I invited beauty

I invited love

We danced on the threshold…close enough to make a hasty retreat –

in case I failed them

When I woke this morning they were there waiting for me –

watching the birds.

And So, We Begin

Tender the new beginning.

A year, a day – a breath –

changing the course of a lifetime.

It slips its hand in mine –

Shall we?

First Night

For tonight the oppressors are absent,

perhaps tormenting another soul.

Your homeless nights have ended.

The power will not be turned on till morning.

Just as well…the candlelight is comforting –

sketching your body in soft curves on the wall.

You've grown comfortable with your own good company.

Curled up in the fresh promise of new sheets,

you wrap your arms around your naked body

warmed by the knowledge of the courage and peril

endured to take this ground.

Strength exhausted; sleep comes quickly –

wrapped in your own embrace.

Set to Rights

Little Sparrow

feel your wings catch the breeze –

your slender legs light upon that heavy branch.

In the sweet soothing shade

slowly you gather yourself

build a cozy nest –

no cage in sight.

Do Not Touch

My soul rises upon the thermals of a pulsating fever.

Heightened inspiration transports

to a world inaccessible without wings.

Do not ground me – capture – or scold.

TOUCH NOT THESE WINGS!

They may be the only ones I get.

Making for Home

Slogging to the crest of the hill

boots heavy with the drag of my muddy pursuit,

drizzle obscures the long view

dampening my optimism.

There's no advantage to the high ground –

there's only keeping on with the thing.

Lost or found – is there a difference?

Do I see home…

or just another familiar turn of the road?

Ease

The Bachelor's velvet antlers saunter,

lingering, savoring

the softness in the air.

Lying in the ebbing summer undergrowth

shaded by expiring cottonwood leaves,

his moist quivering muzzle perceives the changes in fragrance –

the stillness of nature winding down to rest.

The Parting

This day – this day has come.

Fall has come to Our Garden.

We meet to divide the treasures we lovingly assembled.

Gardeners dividing the fading plants

to root them again in separate beds –

hopeful the season of vibrant blooms will come again.

Truce?

Silence like a hiltless dagger…with each thrust both lie bleeding.

Too Tight

My skin is too tight today.

The light too bright…voices too loud

tears too close…understanding too elusive –

no place to be unseen or silence enduring enough

to restore the simple self.

Always the next

                And the Next

                              And the NEXT.

Turbulence distorts connection.

My beleaguered, overstuffed mind masticating

while Time, the all-powerful dominatrix,

binds with cords of doubt, inviting death by tiny cuts.

Opinion's minions stifle the joy of abandon,

conspiring to coerce acceptance.

My skin is too tight today.

Sleight of Hand

Your eyes bruise me.

Silently, carefully,

I fold my petals back over my soul and curl in upon myself.

Brutal and callous the world I see through your eyes –

giving permit to the monster who feeds upon the sacred flesh of women.

Reasoning, tempting,

you seduce her to expose her secrets…

make her common for the purpose of your own lust and greed –

to satisfy your curiosity

to sell your wares.

You convince her this is freedom,

making her a slave to your approval and appetites.

Let Me Entertain You

Okay, I'll crawl inside that party dress

Hide behind a distant smile

Close the blinds behind these eyes

So that you can pretend a while…

Sweet Rebellion

Surrounded by profound forces I cannot comprehend,

true seclusion is but a sweet memory from a distant past.

Penetration perpetrated from all sides –

I am poked and prodded to provoke a response,

then measured, recorded and deposited,

like one more digital fecal sample.

Artistry reduced to a commodity

sold to the highest bidder,

its flame of sincerity and guts removed –

too dangerous, too messy.

Time has been ripped from its lofty status as the Caller of the Dance,

in favor of one sugary injection of instant gratification after another,

mimicking a long-gone sensation of living and contentment.

Pawns survey a menu of choices so vast it impersonates free will.

Yet, in the over-reach they reveal their hand.

Resisting the bondage of oily, seductive, vain promises

I answer a deeper call to live free –

to root again in the slow daily existence of

the rich, mundane life that sustains me.

Rebellious – this simple sweet life.

Quashed Coup

Disquieted, my consciousness

haggles with the purveyors of numbness

while the devious saboteur

breeches lax defenses,

filling all space with concrete.

Awakened by the throes of suffocation,

I eject the intruder.

Free in this beautiful, vibrant, nurturing

breadth of wilderness.

Earth Mother

Shoulders broad

bear this heart's weight.

My head rests in your palm

as your soft steady rain soothes –

hushing the unspeakable,

stirring blooms to release their tranquil fragrance,

as you pull your velvet covers over me –

weaving me once again into this collective beauty.

Communion

The devotion in the fading echo of the Brother's chant,

The cry of passion from the Tenor's soul,

The deep, husky cello vibrating through my body,

The purity of breath in the solitude of a cathedral of trees –

These are like a shared heartbeat.

You are there…I am forgotten and at peace.

Reset

Solitude.

A sensual mystery

excoriating stubborn barnacles

to expose a fresh response

rooted in trust from within.

Freeze Frame

I walk upon frozen snow –

the texture of elephant hide.

Thin crisp crunch –

closest this soul will come to walking on water.

Overhanging rocks above –

a wedge of frost away from rolling destruction.

Overnight the plummeting mercury

creates transparent ribbon-candy wafers of ice.

Autumn's leaves entombed beneath –

preserved in living color.

All that would matter is silenced –

Suspended in the cold…for now.

Hard Lesson

The Specter ridicules trust

wails against the possibility,

indeed…hisses that it is but a trap!

Familiar this darkness.

Cold and understood.

Taught to trust no one…

I carry the sorrow that neither could I you.

I am wedged between the desire to love

and Fear's cold grip upon my hips…

frigid breath upon my throat.

Proof of Life

Quench my thirst in this dry and lonely land

Offer me a drink with the turn of your head

Make your eyes meet mine

Place me here in time.

Resist the droning of the machine

Drowning out voices

Beating hearts

Pulsating blood.

The hairs of my flesh stand at attention

In recognition of another live soul.

Samaritan

Unforeseen, you appeared like an outpost in the wilderness.

With quiet compassion, you walked beside me,

believing in the journey and this resolute traveler.

Unobtrusively, you cleared obstacles,

giving solitude, encouragement, kindness, warmth.

All I have to offer in return is to call you Friend.

Shadow Life

Cocooned in down,

boots kicking fluff before me,

I walk a pristine trail rimmed by fresh shimmering snow

like the glitter trim on a vintage greeting card.

Below, steam rises from the warming pond

and the backs of grazing cattle.

Laughter escapes in frosty gusts

as the sunrise warms my swollen cheeks and lips.

The long-awaited sun returns…and with it,

on the cliff wall at my back – my shadow.

Tattered

Abandoned weathered nests,

dangling misshapen in snow tattered reeds,

rendered uninhabitable by winter's icy onslaught –

feathered winter ghost town.

Secret

Each touch of your strong hands

Deep vibration of your voice

Warm opening of your arms

Draws from deep within a secret hope –

Unspoken.

Pleasures

JOY…not a resounding hallelujah,

more like that favorite worn-soft pair of kick-back blue jeans,

reminding the wearer of other simple comforts…

Warm feet. Secure shelter. Hot soup. Kind friends.

Rich coffee. Savory food. Sunrise. Sunset.

Kisses. Burning embers. Deep baths.

Music. Touch. Laughter.

All

Better

When

Shared.

Mystic Morning

Coaxed from slumber by soft morning light,

reluctant lashes shake off sleep.

The muffled notes of winter

pull me to the window.

What is this mystery…

that after such an arduous,

protracted pilgrimage

over unpredictable terrain –

I should gaze upon my garden blanketed with snow…

and see a broad spring meadow in bloom?

Turn, Turn, Turn

Folding back on itself in ever increasing layers,

like the ruffles of a Flamenco dancer's dress,

Time sweeps me off my feet.

Locked in its pungent, intimate embrace,

the dance becomes so intricate, so consuming,

it is impossible to retrace my steps…to capture a moment.

Regrets, though heavy, do nothing to slow the turn.

Wistful silences punctuate the driving syncopation,

allowing brief glimpses over my shoulder.

My darlings, my beautiful quartet –

our dance was the sweetest.

Tucked away, seemingly hidden from Time,

suspended in the rising arc of the music –

your innocence a sweet illusion that we had forever.

Unsustainable, the beat must go on.

No stopping and starting from the top.

Open your eyes my darlings –

lean into every turn.

Match Time step for step

thrilled to laughter!

Musings

Like an old man's whiskers

the expired grey grasses

define the contour of the trail

backlit by the morning sun,

while nearby tall flaxen fronds

flit and flirt with the breeze

in disheveled delight.

Nature's Retreat

Remote. Mysterious.

This wandering path

sparingly reveals secrets with every turn.

Compelling. Refreshing.

Each footfall shaking loose the congestion in my mind…

easing and deepening my shallow, rapid breathing.

Nature's retreat from the cold

leaves behind a comforting silence,

unveils its texture in light and shadow,

A rest for eye and body…

while under the frozen surface,

Life idles…preparing to roar.

Tender Trust

Long ago buried

Frozen deep within this prickly crust – it shivers now.

Loosely held in your warm hands – it thaws.

The Biding

Sweet emergent shoots

reaching for the sun,

piercing through packed trodden earth

softened by the melting snow –

Patience.

The season's warmth may not yet sustain you.

Awaken in your roots

protect your reserves

your time will come…

Spring Lamb

Just born out of the darkness

lying steaming upon the frozen ground

craving warmth for the first time.

Alive, but still wrapped in the slick diaphanous membrane

that once encapsulated and sustained your life –

you pant from an exhausting journey.

Thrashing…tearing through,

fighting to fill your lungs, pump your blood,

free your legs to stand.

The now spent organ shrivels

in the persistent radiance of the spring sun –

 Step away.

Sing to Me

The thunder told me it was morning.

Soft rain and bird song drew me out into

the damp chill of a new beginning.

Prancing upon the pebbled path

Sweet Robin pulls a smile to my lips.

Raindrops in the laundry room bucket concern me not –

my garden sings!

Magnificent One

Standing

Face lifted

Feet bare

Heart free

I hear the bird's morning song of joy

and respond in kind.

Oh, sweet bird of song,

we are not the tree.

Our delicate resilient wings

catch the breeze and

keep us free to rise…and fall,

with equal passion

to unleash the songs of sorrow and joy –

songs that wake the soul in the morning

and sustain us through the coming night.

Magnificent Valiant Tree,

where would we learn and come to know love,

if not in the liberty and shelter of your

ever reaching branches?

How could we soar without your intrepid roots?

Author Bio

Jeanine Renée is a poet and singer songwriter. *Railwalker,* her first published collection of poems, emerged from her connection to the rhythms of the dirt roads and rail tracks she wanders. Jeanine, a touring songwriter, loves performing at small theatres, festivals, and house concerts. Jeanine makes her home in the small town of Paonia, Colorado with her husband, Lou.

Booking Information

Jeanine enjoys connecting with the audience at her events, telling the stories behind her poems and songs. What motivates her to travel are the folks she meets and the tales collected along the way. To contact her to speak and/or perform at your local bookstore, book club, house concert or other event, please do so at: jeanine@tarpapermedia.com.

Lonesome Road and I

Tonight I walk this old ditch road
Where I know I'm out of sight
Where I can feel that freight train coming
Where the stars light up the sky

And when that train rolls through like thunder
I want to climb right up inside
Steel wheels and clanging couplers
Drown out the chatter in my mind.

I gotta walk this road alone, Its the only way I know
To ease my troubled mind, lift the burden on my soul

(Excerpt from Jeanine's album *Plastic Madonna* released May 2023, available at jeaninerenee.bandcamp.com)

www.ingramcontent.com/pod-product-compliance
Lightning Source LLC
LaVergne TN
LVHW041230080426
835508LV00011B/1143